EVIDENCE

WHAT IS HISTO

Jon Nichol

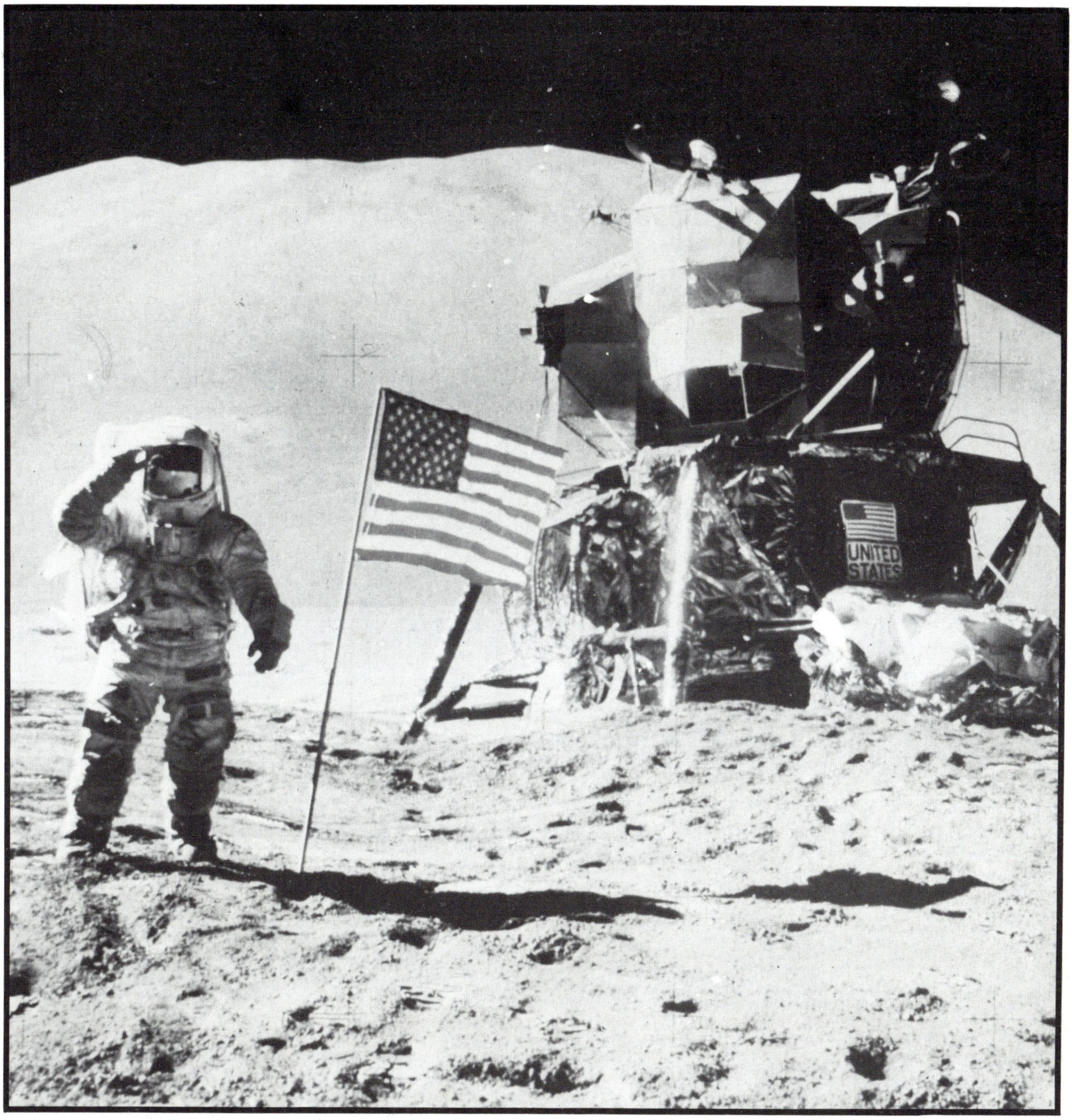

Basil Blackwell · Oxford

CONTENTS

Introduction	3
The bodies in the bog History is about detective work	4-5
Men, women, families, groups and nations History is about people in the past	6-7
Tinker, tailor, soldier, sailor . . . History is about all kinds of people in the past	8-9
Rich man, poor man, beggarman, thief History is about what people thought, felt, and did	10-11
Father Time History is about people in past time	12-13
King Arthur 1: secondary sources History is about finding out from second-hand sources	14-15
King Arthur 2: primary sources History is about finding out from first-hand clues or evidence from the time; written and spoken (oral) evidence	16-17
King Arthur 3: primary sources Archaeological evidence	18-19
Sutton-Hoo: the mystery of the burial mound Clues have problems: missing clues, difficult clues	20-21
Murder? the Princes in the Tower: primary and secondary sources Clues have problems: conflicting clues	22-23
Who burnt down the school? Using clues to recreate the past	24-25
History around us: our house History is about asking questions	26-27
History around us: our school	28-29
History around us: the Second World War	30-31
Quiz time	32

INTRODUCTION

A historian finds out what he can about men and women in the past. To do this, he asks questions about people. Let us take a simple question. What is the person like who sits next to you? To find out, empty your pockets or satchel, and put its contents in front of you. Exchange your pile with your neighbour's. List what is in his or her pile. Then say what these clues tell you about him or her. Use these questions to help you.

1. What is he like?
2. What interests him?
3. What has he done or may do?
4. Where does he live?
5. How does he get to school?

What is History? looks at how we study the past. History is made up of what people did, and how they did it. To find this out, *historians* sort out clues or *evidence* which the past has left behind. This book explains how you can begin to do your own history.

Pages 4-5 suggest that a historian works like a detective in the way he thinks about the past's clues or *evidence*. On pages 6-11 you get an idea of the different kinds of men and women in history. Pages 12-13 show how we measure *time* in the past, and use it to put the facts of history into order. On pages 14-15 we start to handle simple historical *evidence* — in this case what you read in history books. Pages 16-19 examine some of the many types of first-hand historical clues about the past. Pages 20-25 point out some of the problems which you will face when you work on clues from history. They suggest how you might sort out your ideas and reach conclusions. Pages 26-31 suggest

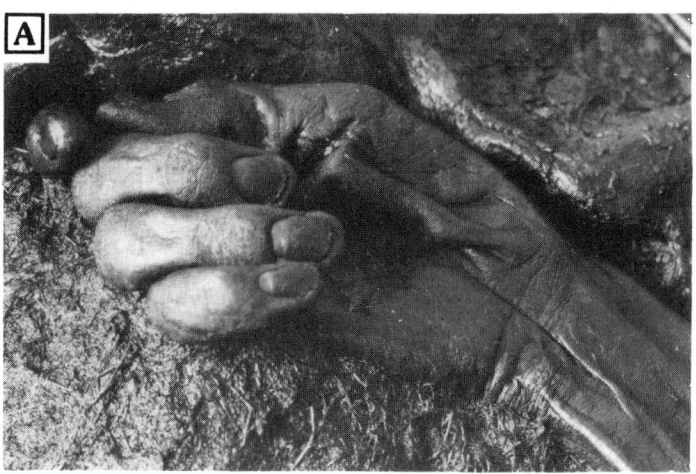

some of the kinds of history you can do — for example, the story of your house, of your school, and of your area during the Second World War.

The book is set out for class, group or work by single pupils. The questions are in rough order of hardness. They allow you to work at your own speed.

Historians use *evidence* from the past to write the history you read in books. The historian is like a detective who hunts out clues and then pieces them together to find out what went on. **A** is a clue from history — can you see what it is? After each point, **a, b, c,** add any new thoughts and ideas you might have about the *clue*.

a The hand is from the body of a dead man who was found buried in a peat bog.
b The corpse was as naked as the day it was born — without a stitch of clothing.
c The man had a broken skull.

How, when and why did he die? Pages 2-3 give you more clues about this and other corpses found in bogs in Denmark. History is about asking questions of clues from the past. **A** is the first of many bits of *evidence* we will look at in this book.

THE BODIES IN THE BOG

History is about detective work

A, B and C are the heads of three men whose bodies were found in three bogs in Denmark. D shows a stake which pinned down a living woman. Her corpse was dug out of another bog. Professor P. V. Glob tells us in E how he visited a site where a body had just been found.

E *An early spring day — 8 May 1950. Dusk was falling over Tollund Fen in Bjaeldskov valley (Denmark). For a second the sun shone, bright yet low in the sky. Like magic it brought things to life. The quiet evening was only broken now and again by the harsh call of a snipe. Deep down in the dark brown peat the dead man, too, seemed to have come alive. He lay on his damp bed as though asleep, resting on his side. The head leaned forward a little, and his arms and legs were bent. On his face was a gentle look — the eyes tight shut, the lips softly closed as if in quiet prayer. It was as though the dead man's soul had come back for a moment from another world, through that gate in the clouds . .*

. . A few hours earlier the dead man had been brought out from the shelter of the peat by two men. Their spring sowing was over, so they now had to think of the cold winter days to come. They were

A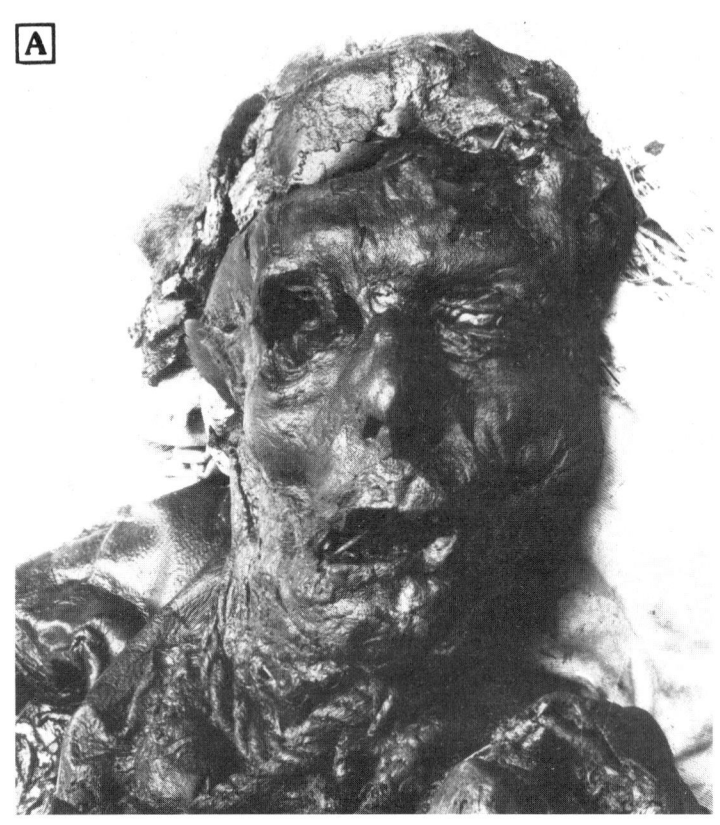

B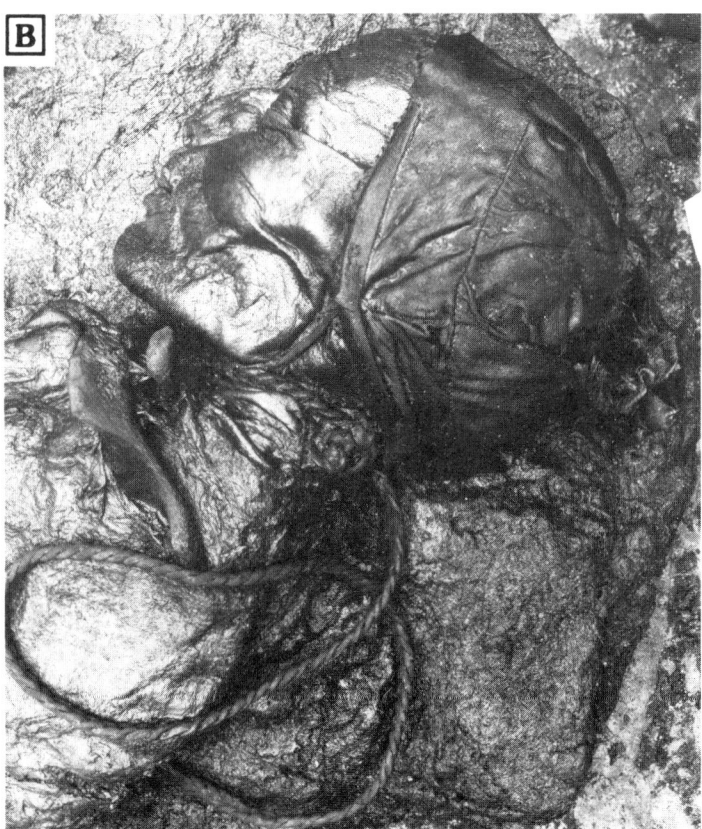

C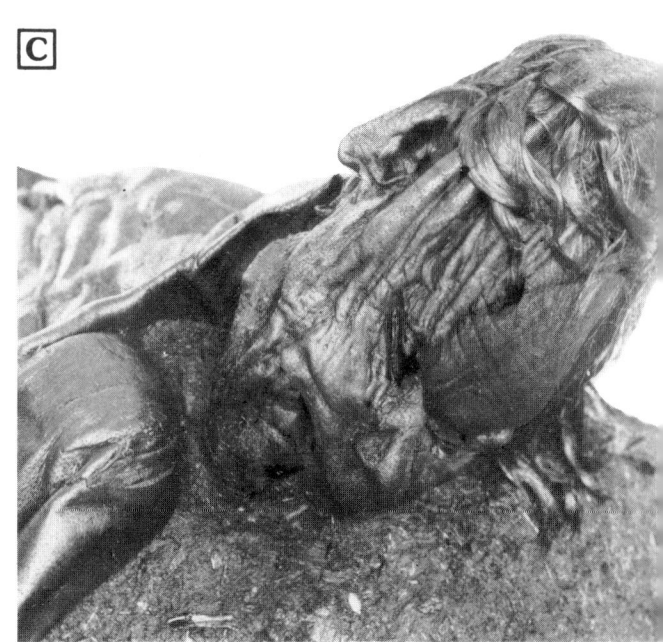

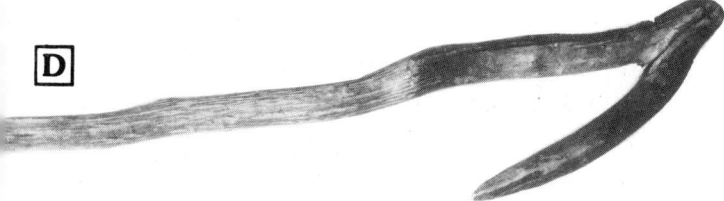

D

busy cutting peat for the tile stove and the kitchen range. As they worked, they suddenly saw in the layer of peat a face so fresh that they could only think they had found a recent murder. They told the police at Silkeborg, who came to the site at once. The police, however, also asked men from the local museum to go with them. Well kept remains of Iron-Age men were not unknown in central Jutland.

At the site the truth about the body soon became clear. A telephone call was put through straight away to Aarhus University. At that time I was teaching a group of students on archaeological problems. Some hours later—that same evening—I stood with my students bent over the startling find, face to face with . . .

Professor Glob is an archaeologist—he digs up historical clues buried in the ground. He had the bodies put in a kind of vinegar, like pickled onions. They are now on public show in Danish museums. A historian like Professor Glob builds up in his mind a picture of what went on in the past. To do this, he asks *questions* about the *clues—the evidence—*which he finds. Professor Glob asked questions like those in exercise **3** about the bodies in the bogs. By each question are some hints about the kinds of answer you might give.

1 Which of the heads—**A**, **B**, **C**—did Professor Glob see?

2 Fit the right word in the list into each gap:
An . . . . . . is a man who digs up historical clues or . . . . . . The . . . . . asks questions about the clues to build up in his mind a . . . . . . of the past.
Potato; historian; chemist; nonsense; evidence; archivist; archaeologist; present; picture.

3 Copy out these questions, with your answers below each.
  a How did they die?
  Can you see what **A** and **B** have around their necks?
  Can you see what has happened to **C**'s throat.
  What does **D** suggest about the woman's death?

b When did they die?
In the men's stomachs was some food. Scientist's carried out tests on this. The tests showed that the men had been in the bogs from 1500 to 2000 years.
  c Why did they die?
A writer who lived 1800 years ago tells us that the tribes who lived in Denmark drowned men and women in bogs to punish them. Also, they killed people as sacrifices to their gods.

4 In **E** Professor Glob talks about how he first saw head **B**. Pretend you were one of his pupils, with him when he went to see the body. Say how you might have felt. Use these words to help:
  marsh; peat; evening; head; cap; eyes; nose; face; neck; rope; police; murder.

MEN, WOMEN, FAMILIES, GROUPS AND NATIONS

History is about people in the past

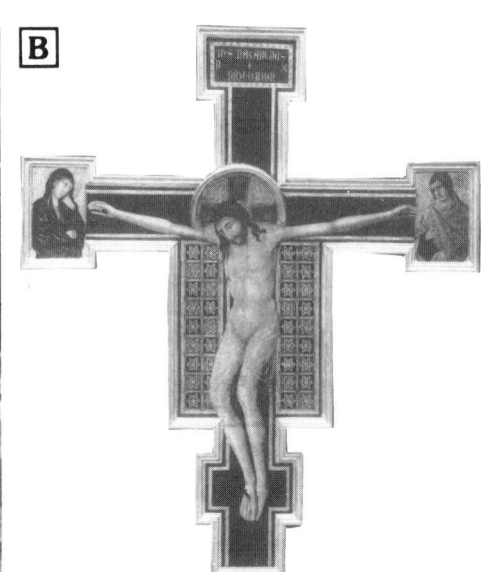

History is about men, women and children who lived in the past. **A**, **B** and **C** show famous people from history—a queen, a holy or religious man, and the ruler of a country. Which picture matches which person? Do you know who they are? If so, how?

History is about families. Much of the history of Britain and its Commonwealth is tied up with the story of a family—**D**. Most families have photographs, letters and stories about their members.

History is about larger groups of people. **E** is a photograph of the pupils of a school about eighty years ago. **F** shows a tribe of Australian aboriginies. Much of history tells what happened to tribes. It is likely that where you now live was the land of a tribe in the Dark Ages (see pages 12-13).

History is about nations and countries, and how they get on together. Television, radio and newspapers inform us about this. **G** is a newspaper headline from December 1941. It tells us of a change in the way Britain and Japan got on during the Second World War (1939-45).

History helps you understand a number of key ideas or concepts. One of these is *change*, and what it means. **G** is about one of the many changes in history.

E

F

G

Oxford Mail

TELEPHONE 4141   MONDAY, 8 DECEMBER, 1941

Britain Declares War On Japan: Speech By Premier

AT a specially-summoned meeting of the Commons this afternoon the Prime Minister announced that the Cabinet, which met at 12 o'clock to-day, was authorised to make a declaration of war on Japan.

Going on to review the dramatic events of the last 24 hours, Mr. Churchill said that the Japanese began the landing in British territory in Northern Malaya about 6 a.m. (1 a.m. local time) yesterday and they were immediately engaged by our forces. (Cheers.)

At home the Home Office measures against Japanese nationals were set in progress at 10.45 last night.

Mr. Churchill drew attention to the fact that some of the finest ships of the Royal Navy had reached their stations in the Far East "at a convenient moment"—a fact on which he was later congratulated by Mr. Hore-Belisha.

The Prime Minister said that the Royal Netherlands Government at once marked their solidarity with Great Britain and the United States at 3 a.m. by stating that as a consequence of Japan's action a state of war now exists between the kingdom of the Netherlands and Japan.

INCREASING OUR HOLD IN LIBYA

Tobruk Again Linked With Sidi Rezegh

THE latest information from Libya indicates that in all sectors our pressure is steadily increasing. A heavy toll is being taken of Axis tanks, transport and supplies.

According to authoritative circles in London, patrols operating from Tobruk have again been able to join hands with our armoured car patrols, which advanced from the south to Sidi Rezegh.

To-day's Middle East war communique from Cairo states:—

"Throughout the whole battle area our pressure is steadily increasing.

"West of Bir-el-Gobi, an enemy force of about 30 tanks and 500 motor vehicles was heavily shelled and attacked by our armoured forces about midday on the 6th, as reported in yesterday's communique.

"In this action seven enemy tanks were destroyed and three enemy tanks and a number of mechanical transport damaged.

??????????

1 Match *one* of sources **A–G** with *one* of **a–d**:
 a photograph of the British Royal Family in Jubilee Year—1977;
 b photograph of Hitler;
 c painting of Queen Victoria;
 d painting of Jesus Christ.
Say why you made your choices.

2 What does **E** tell you about the children it shows?

3 Name the people in **D**. Which of them are: grandparents, parents, grandchildren?

4 Fill in a table like this, giving the date of each source **A–G**.

Source	Date
A	
B	
C	
D	
E	
F	
G	

5 What does **G** tell you about the change in relations between Japan and Britain in 1941?

6 Tell of one change which has happened to your family in the past five years, and what it means.

TINKER, TAILOR, SOLDIER, SAILOR...

History is about all kinds of people in the past

History studies all kinds of people. **A–H** show many different kinds of men and women from history. These pictures are clues about how they lived and what they were like.

A second key idea or concept you get from history is *continuity*—how things tend to stay the same, with only a few changes. Many of the jobs shown in **A–H** are still done, some in the same way.

E

F

G

H

??????????

1 **A–H** show these people:
beggar; factory workers; kitchen servant; nun; farm workers; shopkeeper; smiths; soldier.
Say which picture shows which kind of person. Say why you made your choice.

2 Look at one of the people, and describe him or her in detail. Say:
how he makes a living;
how he is dressed;
what kind of person he is.

3 Make up a story as if the person you have chosen was telling you about a day in his life or something exciting which happened to him.

4 List the jobs in **A–H** that are done today, and say how they have stayed the same, and how they have changed.

RICH MAN, POOR MAN, BEGGARMAN, THIEF

History is about what people thought, felt and did

A—G are scenes from history. Can you work out what they are? Each shows a different side of life in the past: for example, fighting or farming.

Two more key ideas we understand through history are *cause*—why things happen, and *consequence*—the results. For example, The Normans* explains what led up to scene **A**, and what were its short-term and long-term results.

*Jon Nichol, *The Normans*, Basil Blackwell, 1980

???????????????????????????????

1 Sources **A–G** show people doing many kinds of things. Look for the clues in each source, and make out a table like the one below, using lists **a** and **b**. Use the words from list **a** in column 1, those from **b** in column 2. For example do you think **A** is a *miner* who is *cooking*?

Source	1	2
A		
B		
C		
D		
E		
F		
G		

a Kitchen servant, soldiers, astronaut, child miners, sportsmen, schoolchildren/teacher, pilot.

b exploring, working, relaxing, teaching and learning, fighting, inventing, cooking.

2 Which pictures show rich men, poor men?

3 Add to list **b** any other jobs that people have done in the past.

4 Among **A–G** are famous scenes from History. Which pictures show:
   a The first walk on the moon?
   b King Harold's death at the Battle of Hastings?
   c The first flight of an aeroplane?

11

FATHER TIME

History is about people in past time

How do you measure how long it takes an athlete to run: 1500 metres; 100 metres; a marathon? For which of these do you use: seconds; minutes and seconds; hours, minutes and seconds? In each case you are recording *time*.

Table **A** lists some of the ways we measure longer and longer pieces of time. Can you fit into the correct box the terms in the list below?

A Time	How Measured
100 metre-race	
1500 metre-race	
Marathon race	
Time in the morning	
Time in the afternoon	
Time 24 hours ago	
Time several days ago	
Time over seven days ago	
Time over thirty days ago	
Time over 365 days ago	
Time over 3,650 days ago	
Time over a hundred years ago	
Time over several hundred years ago	
Time before Christ's birth	
Time after Christ's birth	

A month; a day; seconds; decade; minutes; hours; AD; BC; centuries; ages—e.g. the Dark Ages; a.m.; p.m.; a year; a week; a past week.

The terms in table **A** help us put facts from the past in their order in time. Take a fact you all know: when you were born. For example, Jim Smith was born at 2.45 am on 21st December 1974. You can show which year you were born on a time line. Draw a line with one centimetre for each year for the last seventeen years, like **B**.

B

1960 1965 1970 1975

Mark on the line when you were born, when you first went to school, and any important things that have happened to you.

You can use the same kind of line to show what major things have happened to your family—parents and grandparents—or people you and they know. Draw a line which starts in 1900, using a centimetre for every five years. Mark in the First and Second World Wars, 1914-1918, 1939-1945, and the important things you can find out about your family or its friends: when they were born, married, worked and retired. **C** shows such a line.

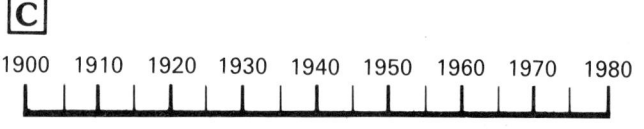

People have always split up the year into *seasons*. We divide our year into four seasons. What do we call them? What season are we in now?

12

When we talk about a fact in the past, we often say it happened in a particular century—for example, the eighteenth. The eighteenth century is the years between 1700 and 1799 AD. The years between 1 and 99 AD are the first century.

In British history, a century often takes the name of the ruling royal family—for example, of the Tudors. Centuries join together into *ages*. **D** gives an idea of the ways we split up time.

What do we mean when we say that Julius Caesar invaded Britain in 55 *BC*, or that Jim Smith was born in 1974 *AD*? BC means Before Christ, AD (short for the Latin *Anno Domini*) means After Our Lord. Other people use different points in the past from which to date events—for example, the Muslims. Year 1 in their calendar is 622 AD, when their religion began. What is the present year in the Muslim calendar?

D Ages	Periods	Date	Century
	Greek	400 BC	Fifth BC
		300 BC	Fourth BC
		200 BC	Third BC
		100 BC	Second BC
Classical		1 BC	First BC
	Roman	1 AD	First AD
		100 AD	Second AD
		200 AD	Third AD
		300 AD	Fourth AD
		400 AD	Fifth AD
		500 AD	Sixth AD
	Anglo-saxon	600 AD	Seventh AD
		700 AD	Eighth AD
Dark		800 AD	Ninth AD
	Saxon	900 AD	Tenth AD
		1000 AD	Eleventh AD
	Norman	1100 AD	Twelfth AD
Middle	Angevin	1200 AD	Thirteenth AD
	Plantagenet	1300 AD	Fourteenth AD
	Lancastrian	1400 AD	Fifteenth AD
	Tudor	1500 AD	Sixteenth AD
	Stuart	1600 AD	Seventeenth AD
Modern	Georgian/Hanoverian	1700 AD	Eighteenth AD
	Regency	1800 AD	Nineteenth AD
	Victorian	1840 AD	
	Edwardian	1900 AD	Twentieth AD
		1914 AD	

???????????????????????????

1 If a friend tried to sell you a Roman coin with the date 45 BC on it, what would you say to him?

2 We often use important facts in our lives to date things: for example, your mother might say, 'Before you were born, we lived in London'. In Zimbabwe, many tribes date things from the Queen's visit in 1953. What would be your own plan for dating things in the past fifty years?

3 Make out a time line for the past 2000 years (1cm = 100 years). Mark on it these major events in our history.
 a 55 BC Julius Caesar's invasion
 b 43 AD The Roman Conquest
 c 500-800 AD The Dark Ages
 d 1066 AD The Norman Conquest
 e 1450-1500 The Wars of the Roses
 f 1485-1603 The Tudors
 1603-1714 the Stuarts
 g 1837-1901 The reign of Queen Victoria
 h 1939-45 The Second World War
 i 1953- The reign of Queen Elizabeth II

4 In which centuries did **a–i** happen? For example, **d** was in the 11th century.

13

KING ARTHUR 1: SECONDARY SOURCES

History is about finding out from second-hand sources

Whom does picture **A** show? What do you know about him? If you want to find out about someone like him, or an event in history, how do you go about it? One important *source* is what a historian writes. He pieces together his work from what other historians have written, and from first-hand evidence from the past. What a historian writes is called a *secondary* source.

Let us use what a historian wrote in a book to find out about a famous person in history—King Arthur. **B** is taken from a book on King Arthur.

B *Many Britons fled to escape the invaders. They went westwards, into the hills of what are now Cornwall and Devon, Wales, the Lake District and south-west Scotland. Some even crossed the seas, to Ireland or Brittany in France. It must have been heartbreaking for them to leave their homes and crops, but even this was better than death or slavery.*

However, in some areas the Britons gathered together and armed themselves. Where this happened the invaders met strong resistance. After perhaps half a century of gradual English settlement there seems to have been a British recovery. About the year 500 we are told that the Britons won a big battle at a place called Mount Badon. The invaders were driven out of a large part of the south Midlands, and their advance seems to have been checked for more than half a century.

According to legend several British victories at this time, including the one at Mount Badon, were inspired by a leader called King Arthur. It is likely that Arthur did in fact exist, but he would not have been much like the king in the famous stories of the Round Table. He would have been a war-chief, admired for his exploits in battle. His followers would not have been splendid knights like Sir Lancelot and Sir Galahad, although they may have fought on horseback. They would have been a band of brave Britons, fighting desperately to save their country from invasion.*

How do you use history books like **B** and other *secondary* sources? You have to take a number of steps.

Step 1 You must ask questions.
History means you have to ask questions. Let us take a simple question about King Arthur: who was he?

Step 2 You must look at a book or books.
You may find the answer to your question or questions in *secondary* sources. **B** is taken from one of the hundreds of books on King Arthur. These books are of many kinds. For example,

*R. J. Cootes, *The Middle Ages*

there are school textbooks, novels and biographies (stories of his life) of him. Some of these sources give much more *evidence* than others. **B** helps you begin to answer the question: who was King Arthur?

Step 3 You must sort out the evidence.
Books may give you all the facts you want. To understand these facts, you must think about:
a difficult words: for example, in **B**, *settlement, legend and knights*;
b facts you do not know: for example, in **B**, the Round Table, Sir Lancelot and Sir Galahad.

Step 4 You must judge the evidence.

Can you trust what each book tells you? When you read a history book, think about:
a who wrote it; is he an expert on that subject?
b what *evidence* has he used? can you find any clues that he has looked at a large number and wide range of sources?
c does anything suggest that the book is biased? Can you trust what it says?

Step 5 You must use the evidence to answer the question.
All the facts from your books combine to help answer your questions. Now we will try to answer our question: who was King Arthur?

????????????????????????????

1 Looking at the evidence.
a Look at **A**. It shows King Arthur as a boy. Write a story about the picture, or describe it. Use these words to help you: boy; boots; cloak; cold; sword; stone; anvil.
b Read **B**. List what it tells us about King Arthur.

Sorting out the evidence.
A: to understand clue **A**, you must know the story behind the picture. To find out, ask your teacher or members of your form, or look in books.
B: to find out what the hard words mean, ask your teacher or use a dictionary. If there are any facts you do not know, can also ask your teacher or look in other books on King Arthur.

Write out all the hard words and facts you did not know. By them, put down what you find out.

Judging the evidence.
Can you trust **A** and **B** as historical *evidence*? Think about these points: **A** is from a modern cartoon film. The film is based on stories about King Arthur written about 700 years after he may have lived.
B is from a school textbook. The writer is a school teacher who is not an expert on King Arthur.

Say how much trust you can put in each source, **A** and **B**.

Using the evidence to answer the questions.
Use the evidence on these pages to say who you think King Arthur was. Note the points on which sources **A** and **B** agree and disagree.

2 Historians base their writing upon many sources—books, pamphlets and articles. By **B**, say what sources the historian might have used in his work. work.

3 List the books, **w—z**, in the order in which you would trust what they say.
w *A novel* for children, by a novelist who spends his time reading books on Arthur and his age.
x A university lecturer's *special study* of Arthur.
y A *school textbook* by a history teacher for 11-14 year-olds on Arthur's time.
z A *school textbook* by a history teacher for 16-18 year-olds on King Arthur's time.

KING ARTHUR 2: PRIMARY SOURCES

History is about finding out from first-hand clues or evidence from the time; written and spoken (oral) evidence

The historian put down his books. An interesting topic—what a pity there were so few clues to go on. Only his name—Arthur. No body, not a thing he owned. But this was not so odd, as he had been dead for over 1400 years. The man was King Arthur, leader of the British fighters against the Anglo-Saxon invaders who came to Britain after AD 400.

It should have been a simple problem. The more the historian looked into it, the harder it became. Although everyone has heard of Arthur, there was so little *evidence*. There were a few clues written at the time of Arthur, or soon after. These first-hand pieces of evidence are called *primary* sources.

A British monk, Gildas, wrote the best-known one. In **A**, Gildas tells us about the Anglo-Saxon invasion in about the year that he was born—AD 515.

A *So that they* (the Britons) *should not all be killed, they took up weapons. Under Ambrosius Aurelanius (a Roman) they decided to fight their enemies. He was a modest man, who alone of the Romans chanced to survive the shock of such a storm (the Anglo-Saxon invasion)... To his men, the Lord's help gave victory.* (Ambrosius died but the Britons went on fighting.) *From that time, sometimes the Britons and sometimes their enemies won... This went on up to the year of the siege of Mount Badon, the last great killing of the murderous Anglo-Saxon rabble.*

Gildas does not tell us who led the Britons at Mount Badon, but in their halls and huts stories spread about such a leader, called Arthur. About AD 600, a poet at the court of the British King of Rheged (Cumbria) talked in a poem about a warrior's bravery:

B *Although he was no Arthur...*

Some two hundred years later, in about AD 800 we have the first written life of King Arthur. Nennius, a welsh monk, wrote:

C *Arthur (a soldier) fought against the Saxons with the Kings of the Britons, and led them in battles. The first was at the mouth of the River Glein... The eighth was by Castle Guinnion, in which Arthur carried on his shoulders a picture of the Virgin Mary... The twelfth was on Mount Badon, in which, on that day alone, nine hundred and sixty men fell when Arthur attacked. Alone he killed them. He won all his battles.*

Before a historian uses sources like **A** and **C** to write his own history, he takes a number of steps. Take **D** as an example. It is a clue about whether Cadbury Castle, Somerset, was King Arthur's home.

D *At the very south ende of the chirch of South-Cadbyri standith Camallate, sumtyme a famose toun or castelle, apon a very torre or hille, wunderfully enstrengtheid of nature. In the upper parte of the coppe of the hille be 4 diches or trenches, and a balky waulle of yerth betwixt every one of them . . . Much gold, sylver and coper of the Romaine coynes hath be found ther yn plouing . . . The people can telle nothing ther but that they have hard say that Arture much resortid to Camalat.*

(from John Leland, *Itinerary*, written in 1560)

To use this clue, a historian:
  a takes a copy of the original;
  b works out what old-fashioned words and grammar mean eg *chirch, sumtyme*;
  c find out what words that we no longer use mean—eg *coppe*;
  d looks in books to discover historical points—eg *Roman coins*; *Arthur much resorted (went) to Camelot*;
  e discovers what he can about the source—in this case, who wrote it? When? Can we trust what he says?

The historian working on King Arthur has to ask questions about his primary sources. If you were writing about Arthur, what questions would you ask of **A—D**? There are many other kinds of primary source: for example, photographs, paintings, carvings, buildings, and archaeological remains. Around you are millions of first-hand clues from history—such as family and street names, and things your family owns, like old postcards, letters and magazines.

---

1 Write out this passage, putting in the right word from the list underneath.
A historian uses clues from the time to write his own . . . . These clues or . . . . are called . . . . sources. There are many kinds of primary sources, for example . . . . (secondary, lemon, rubbish, history, primary, history books, evidence, paintings)

2 Primary sources give us facts and ideas. Under a heading for each source, **A—D**, say what it tells us about King Arthur.

3 The historian asks many questions about his sources. Questions **a—d** are on each source, **A**, **B**, **C** and **D**.

  a Do we know for sure that Gildas is talking about Arthur?
  b Why did the poet in **B** mention Arthur?
  c Does anything in **C** suggest that Nennius is lying? If so, what?
  d How important did the writer of **D** think King Arthur was?

4 What did Nennius mean when he said, 'Arthur carried on his shoulders a picture of the Virgin Mary'?

5 Add to your story about Arthur any new ideas or facts you have discovered.

6 Write out **D** in your own words. Do you think **D** is really a primary source?

KING ARTHUR 3: PRIMARY SOURCES

Archaeological evidence

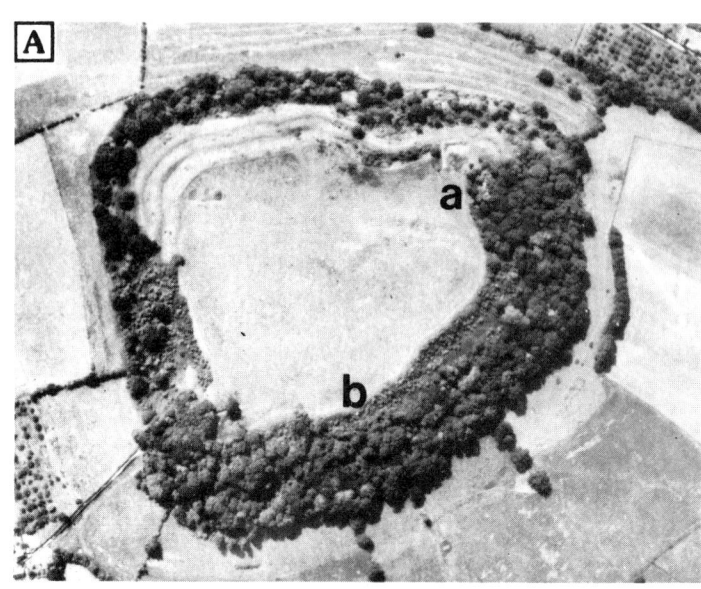

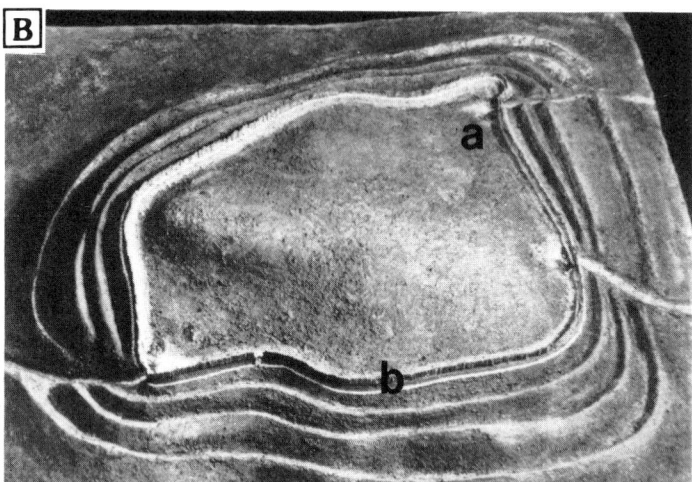

The historian also had some clues about King Arthur that *archaeologists* (see pages 4-5) had found. Their evidence came from Cadbury Castle, Somerset. Cadbury Castle is a hill fort. Local legends say that this was the site of 'King Arthur's palace'. Near the hill fort is the village of Queen Camel, or Camelot. The ancient tales about King Arthur that we looked at on pages 16-17 talk about Camelot. Was Cadbury Castle where Arthur built a palace? The only way to find out if a British leader like Arthur had lived at Cadbury was to dig up the site. Archaeologists did so in 1966 and 1967.

A is a photograph taken from a plane showing the main walls—ramparts—of Cadbury Castle. **B** is a model of how the hill fort might have looked. The archaeologists worked at **a** and **b**. At **a** they found a stony bank built on top of old Roman defences. It is likely that a strong wooden fence stood on the bank. Above the stony bank the Saxons built a stone wall. Using **D** on pages 12-13, say

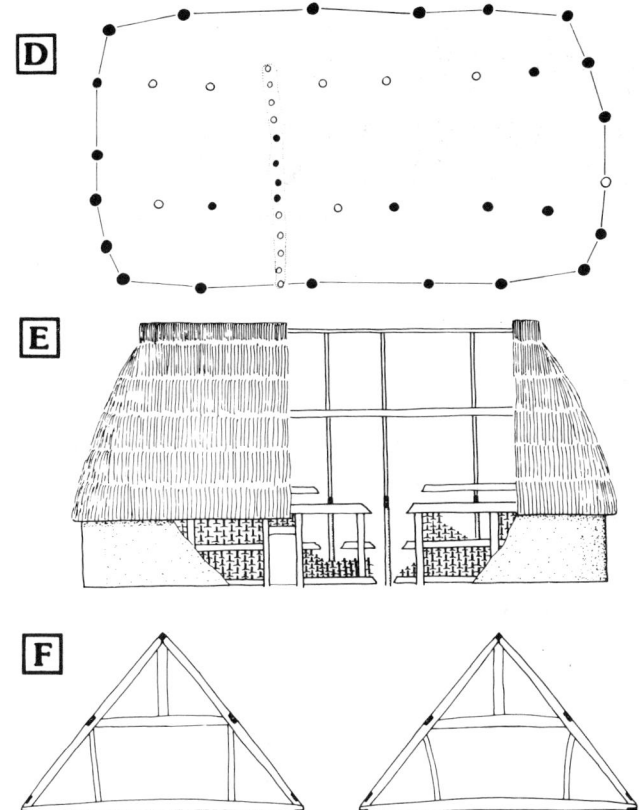

King Arthur's time—AD 500. **D** is a plan of the hall. Historians drew pictures **E** and **F**, with the help of evidence from other excavations, and from stories, poems, tapestries and carvings about halls in the Dark Ages (see pages 12-13). An artist drew **G**, showing life in a hall.

As a historian, you will work on many different kinds of primary source. In studying King Arthur, we have looked at only a few kinds. If you study a modern topic, you will have many more—for example, films, tape recordings, photographs, newspapers, letters, the memories of living people.

when the stone bank and wooden fence were put up.

The stony bank is strong evidence that Cadbury Castle was used as a fort during Arthur's time. At **b** the archaeologists cleared the hill top. **C** is a photograph of the site. The white markers stand where thick wooden posts have rotted away. The archaeologists think that these wooden posts were the supports for a large, wooden hall. They carried out scientific tests on the rotten wood. These tests showed that the hall was built in

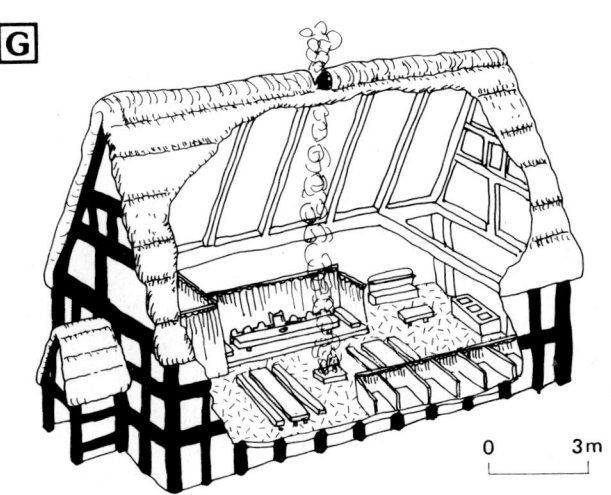

??????????

1 Look at **C**. Why do archaeologists think that a hall was built on this site? What else might the posts have been used for?

2 Which of **i**–**v** made archaeologists think that King Arthur could have lived at Cadbury Castle?
   i rumours and legends;
   ii place names;
   iii written evidence;
   iv earlier archaeological finds;
   v guesswork.

3 The historian uses his *imagination* to recreate from the evidence what the past *might* have been like. Use model **B** either to trace or to draw your plan of the hill fort's defences. Put in the gate, **c**, and fence, **d**. Then say how many defenders it would have needed if a band of one hundred Anglo-Saxon warriors attacked it, and what problems would have faced the attackers.

4 Say what the evidence **A–G** tells you about the British chief who lived at Cadbury Castle.

19

SUTTON HOO: THE MYSTERY OF THE BURIAL MOUND

Clues have problems: missing clues, difficult clues

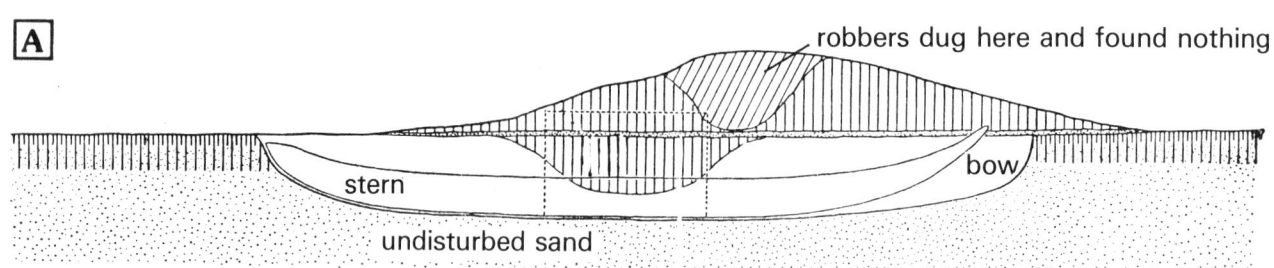

Plan of the Sutton-Hoo mound from the side

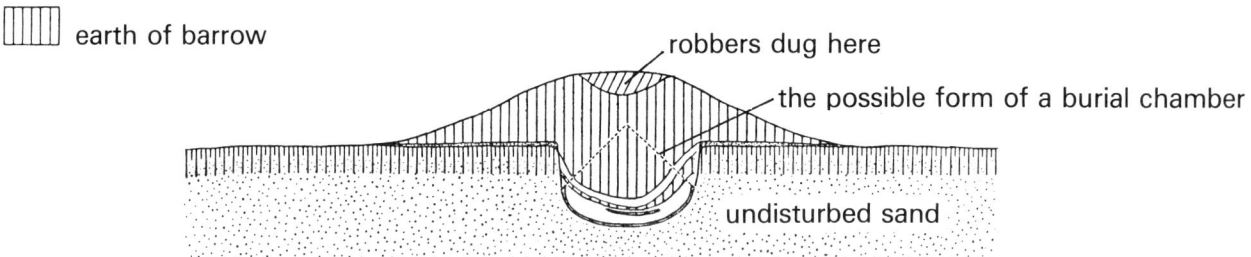

Plan of the Sutton-Hoo mound from the front

The archaeologists' dig—excavation was over. They had removed all the treasures from the burial mound at Sutton Hoo, near Woodbridge, Suffolk. **A** is a plan of the mound, and **B** is a photograph of what the archaeologists found at its bottom. The impression in the earth is where wood has rotted away. Can you see what was buried in the ground?

From clues that the archaeologists found in the burial mound, they worked out that it was dug in Anglo-Saxon times (see pages 10-11). **B** clearly shows where a ship was laid at rest. Evidence from other sources gives us an idea of what the ship was like. An Anglo-Saxon poem, *Beowulf*, tells us that its hero:

C ... *left the land of the Danes in his*

D

ship to plough the deep water. A rope tied a sea-cloth, the sail, to the mast. The boat stayed on course while its timbers creaked and the wind blew it over the waves. With foam around its neck, the seafarer went on its way, its clinker-built bows slicing the ocean path.

The poet said that the ship was 'newly tarred' and had 'carved bows'. A historian drew a picture of what the ship might have looked like—**D**. He used the evidence in the mound, and all that he could find out about Anglo-Saxon ships from sources like *Beowulf*.

???????????????????????????

1 Use **B** to say:
   a how many planks did the ship have down each side?
   b how many ribs did the ship have?
   c how wide was the ship?
   d how deep was it at the middle?
   e how were the planks fixed to the ribs?

2 Use the evidence on these pages to draw a plan of the ship. On it show:
   f the mast
   g a steering oar
   h seats for oarsmen

3 The Sutton Hoo ship could sail in 70 cm of water. With its oars, where could it travel?

4 The Sutton Hoo ship was of no use as a warship. Can you think why? The plank marks in the soil showed that it had been heavily repaired. What kind of ship might it have been, and what would have been its uses?

5 Why do historians think that the Sutton Hoo ship had features **f** to **h**? None of them was shown by the impression in the ground.

6 Historians use evidence from the past to recreate how things have been. Think about the evidence on these pages, and anything you can find out from books about the Sutton Hoo ship and other Anglo-Saxon ships. Then describe how the boat might have looked, and what it might have been like to have sailed in it from Denmark to Sutton Hoo *or* Make a model of the Sutton Hoo Ship.

MURDER? THE PRINCES IN THE TOWER:
primary and secondary sources

Clues have problems: conflicting clues

One of history's great mysteries is what happened to the Princes in the Tower. They were the two sons of King Edward IV (1461-83). Edward died in April 1483, when his older boy was twelve, and his younger ten. The elder child was too young to rule by himself, and so his uncle Richard ran the country for him. In July 1483, Richard seized the throne and was crowned King Richard III.

Richard had many rivals among England's nobles. Two of these were the Duke of Buckingham and Henry Tudor. In 1485 Henry came back to England from abroad, raised an army and killed Richard III at the Battle of Bosworth, 22nd August 1485.

By 1486 the two sons of King Edward IV had clearly disappeared. Indeed, no one had seen them since July 1483, and there were many rumours about what had happened to them. **A—F** are six pieces of evidence about the fate of the Princes in the Tower.

A *When King Edward IV died in April 1483, the Duke of Gloucester (Richard III) wrote most kind letters to comfort the Queen. He promised to obey and be loyal to his brother's oldest son, who was to become King Edward V and said he would set out for London right away. He and his men arrived in York in mourning dress, and there he held a solemn and very sad service in memory of his brother . . .*

Richard was crowned as king.

A is from a primary source of the time, the *Croyland Chronicle*. We think John Russell, Bishop of Lincoln, wrote the chronicle. He was Richard III's chief minister, and worked very closely with him from 1483.

B *Tyrell decided that the Princes should be murdered in their beds the next night, and chose Miles Forest and John Dighton to do the job. Forest was one of the Princes' guards and had already murdered others; Dighton was a big, broad, strong fellow. About midnight they entered the chamber where the children lay asleep in their beds. They pressed the feather beds and pillows hard on the children's faces until they stopped breathing, and fetched Sir James Tyrell to see them . . .*

This story is well known to be true, because when Sir James Tyrell was imprisoned in the Tower in 1502 for treason against King Henry VII, both he and Dighton were questioned. They confessed that they had done the murder in the way I have described.

B is taken from Sir Thomas More's *History of King Richard III*. It tells how Sir James Tyrell had the Princes murdered after July 1483. Sir Thomas claims that Sir James acted on the orders of Richard III, who sent him with a letter to the warden of the Tower of London. The letter ordered the warden to give Sir James the keys of the Tower for a day. The Princes lived in the Tower, which was a royal palace as well as a prison.

Sir Thomas More wrote **B** in 1513. He lived in the court of Henry VII's son,

E

Henry VIII (1509-47), and had been brought up as a member of the family of John Morton, Archbishop of Canterbury. Morton hated Richard III, who had imprisoned him for plotting against him in 1483.

C *It will perhaps come as a surprise to the reader used to the firm claims of history texts and guidebooks that there is no proof that King Richard murdered the two sons of King Edward IV. If we take 'evidence' to mean evidence that would secure a verdict in a court of law, there is no evidence that he murdered the princes. Upon what clues, then, must an enquiry be based? — upon rumours and hearsay, assertion from sources of proved unreliability and inaccuracy . . .*

The princes were murdered by the orders of one of three men. It is very possible that King Richard is guilty of the crime. If he is innocent, then it is almost certain that either King Henry VII (Henry Tudor) or Henry Stafford, second Duke of Buckingham, is guilty. . . .

D *Buckingham had means of access to the Tower and to the Princes. It appears that he did not set out with Richard on the royal progress (in 1483), but . . . stayed a few days in London and then overtook Richard at Gloucester. And after he said goodbye to the King, he rode away into Wales to begin plotting his overthrow. He had motives for murdering the Princes which were both stronger and more urgent than the King's. . . .Buckingham, on fire to claim the throne, must get rid of them at once, because they were deadly rivals to his hopes.*

In 1955 Professor Paul Kendall wrote a biography of Richard III. Professor Kendall looked in great detail at all the evidence about the death of the Princes in the Tower. **C** and **D** are extracts from his book, changed slightly so that you can understand them.

Professor Kendall said that the Princes died in the summer of 1483. In 1483 a strong lord, the Duke of Buckingham, led a rising against Richard III. Buckingham might have murdered the Princes.

E shows the murder of the princes, as a Victorian artist imagined it.

? ? ? ? ? ? ? ? ? ? ?

1 Look at each source, **A–E**, and say what it tells us about the fate of the Princes in the Tower. Say for each clue:

a What it tells us about Richard III;
b What it tells us about the end of the Princes;
c What it tells about other people who might have played a part in the Princes' end;
d How much trust you can place in the source.

2 Say what you think happened to the Princes in the Tower.

3 Do you think Richard III was guilty of murdering them?

23

WHO BURNT DOWN THE SCHOOL?

Using clues to recreate the past

Historians use evidence that survives from the past to find things out. **A**, **B** and **C** are from a *log book* like the one kept for your school. A government inspector wrote **A**—it is part of a report on the school. I bought the log in a bookshop. It is the only clue I have about the school and the events described in **B** and **C**.

A

BOARD OF EDUCATION
Local Education Authority
BLACKWELL CAMP SCHOOL FOR GIRLS

Inspected on 9th, 11th and 16th June 1927.
Report by HMI Miss A F Marks and Miss L D Adams.

The Camp School receives batches of 40 to 60 girls from the Birmingham schools for twelve days' residence under instruction.

The generous gift of a shelter and land in a country village some few miles from Birmingham on a spur of the Lickey Hills enabled the Education Authority to start a temporary camp; further gifts have made extension possible and it is now placed on a permanent footing.

The camp consists of a main building with a lawn, flower beds and shrubbery, a night shelter built along two sides of an asphalt square and a field of seven acres. The main building is attractive with its steeply sloping thatched roof, its blue and white woodwork, and its bright orange curtains: it contains a large hall which is used for meals as well as for indoor work and play, and, in addition, the staff room and the kitchen. The sleeping quarters are in a wooden shelter with open window spaces, protected by covered verandas: whilst the general arrangements are very good, the provision for washing is somewhat crude and the lack of sanitary conveniences under the same roof is unfortunate. The field gives ample space for recreation and provides unusually good opportunities for Nature observation.

In the summer season the poorer schools of the City, three at a time, nominate batches of twenty children, from eleven to fourteen years of age; no monetary contribution is required and the preference is given to children who would not otherwise have an opportunity of getting into the country.

B

an Assistant on the Teaching Staff.

April 6th. 35. Entire demolition of Shelter by fire.

At approx. 11.40am, small flame at top of thatched roof in immediate vicinity of kitchen chimney, noticed by child playing outside.

C

April 1st '35
Camp reopened with 57 girls—30 from Bloomsbury Senior Girl's School and 27 from Hope St Senior Mixed.

Miss D M Smith commenced her duties as an assistant on the teaching staff.

April 6th '35
Entire demolition of shelter by fire. At approx 11.40 am, small flame at top of thatched roof in immediate vicinity of kitchen chimney, noticed by child playing outside.

Alarm immediately given to Matron, Miss Tomlinson and 2 maids in kitchen, also to Miss Newey, teacher, with 9 girls in dining-room.

Matron immediately summoned Bromsgrove Fire Brigade, and informed Birmingham Education Committee.

Miss Newey, keeping back smartest girl to race to gardener's cottage, sent the remaining 8 quietly to farthest end of the playground, in which 48 girls were having organised games with Miss Smith, teacher. Miss Newey brought register—the roll was called—every child was present—57. They were left sitting quietly on playground verandah, out of sight of fire, by Miss Newey, Miss Smith remaining in charge.

Meanwhile the Matron and maids secured stepladder, all fire-extinguishers and fire-buckets on premises, and with the help of a few older children, filled every kitchen bucket and bath. A chain of buckets was formed immediately.

In less than 2 minutes, Harry Groves, summoned from Yew Tree Cottage, was on roof, endeavouring to extinguish flame, by then as large as bucket. Helpers supplied him with extinguishers and water. Flames on top were extinguished, but others were discovered fast breaking out inside building, and part of roof was already falling.

The Fire Brigade arrived in 9 minutes from summons. Everything possible was done without the slightest delay, but, owing to prevailing high wind and nature of building materials, the structure was doomed.

The staff-room was cleared of all contents, piano was removed from dining-room, but all else was destroyed.

At 12.20 pm., children packed cases, and were sent home, accompanied by Miss Newey and Miss Smith, who stayed with them until their homes were reached.

Firemen remained until approx. 5 pm, until sure that all danger had been averted.

Cause of fire unknown.

???????????????????????????????

1 Draw up a table like **D** to work out what the school was like.

Where was the school?	
What were its buildings like?	
Who used it?	
How many pupils did it have?	
What was it used for?	

2 What happened on the 6th April 1935?

3 Who might have started the fire?

4 Imagine you were staying at the school on 6th April 1935. In your own words say what happened. Use these words to help you:

playing; kitchen; smoke; flames; Miss Newey; running girl; playground; register; sitting; talking; buckets; fire-fighting; man on roof; fire-engines; piano; packing; ashes.

5 Can we trust what **A**, **B** and **C** tell us?

6 If you wanted to find out more about the fire, how would you go about it?

HISTORY AROUND US: OUR HOUSE

History is about asking questions

A is a picture of our house. I wanted to know when it was built and who lived there in its early years. How could I find out the answers to these questions?

The first step was to visit the *local library.* At the library, where did I start? A good idea was to look at general books—*secondary sources*—on the history of Exeter—for I live at 24 Wonford Road, St Leonard's, Exeter. Each book had a table of contents in front and an index at the back. Using these, I tracked down references to Wonford Road—the street—and St Leonard's—the area. A famous

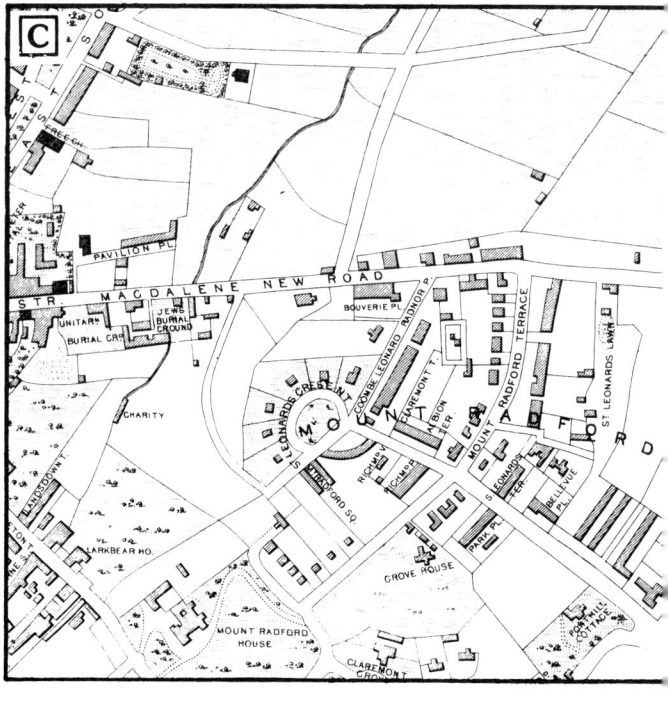

> **B** *A new kind of city*
> Exeter was changing its character rapidly in the first forty years of the nineteenth century. Down to the out break of the French Wars (1793), she had still been an important industrial and commercial city, with a very considerable overseas trade; but the twenty or more years of war and blockade had practically killed all this trade. Despite this heavy blow, the city doubled in size between 1800 and 1840. Why was this?
> At the beginning of the century, Exeter, with its mainly working-class suburb of St Thomas across the river, had just about 20 000 people. Heavitree was still a pleasant little village of a few hundred people to which middle-class citizens who could afford it migrated for a summer holiday and the salubrious country air. The suburb of St Leonard's had not yet come into existence. By the 1840s, the population of the city and its suburbs had increased to some 40 000. Heavitree was now joined to Exeter, not continuously but by large houses in ample gardens, and the suburb of St Leonard's, largely occupied by the families of naval and military men, had come into existence since 1830. It was developed mainly by the big building family of Hooper who bought much of the Baring estate on this side of Exeter in the 1820s.

D *Note* Wonford Road was called Radnor Place in 1851. Our house was No 12.

Name of street, Place, or Road, and Name or No. of House	Name and Surname of each Person who abode in the house, on the Night of the 30th March 1851	Relation to head of family	Age	Condition	Rank, Profession or Occupation	Where born
12 Radnor Place	Frederick Bell	Head	42	M	Chaplain of the City Workhouse	Ireland, Dublin
	Mary Bell	Wife	27	M		Middlesex, London
	Frederick Bell	Son	2	-		Devon, Dawlish
	Wilfred Bell	do.	1	-		Devon, Teignmouth
	Susannah Jewel	Serv.	41	M	General Servant	Devon, Teignmouth
	Sarah Skinner	do.	42	M	do.	Cornwall
	Marianne Sclater	do.	12	U	do.	Devon, Exeter

historian, Professor W. G. Hoskins, wrote one of the books.

When I had sorted out the background facts from Hoskins and other books, I moved on to look at some original evidence—*primary sources*. Which should I choose? Maps seemed a good idea. The librarian found those for 1800-40. **C** shows the first time it appeared on a map in 1835. Our road was then called Combe Leonard Radnor Place.

Who lived in our house? The librarian said that the best place to look was the 1851 Census. Every ten years since 1801, the government has made a list—census—of everyone living in the country. The 1851 Census is very detailed. **D** is the extract for my house.

These sources helped me to answer questions about my house.

You can do the kind of work outlined on these pages to find out about your own house, or any other house or building that interests you. All you have to do is to start asking questions, find out where to look, and think about the evidence you discover.

???????????

1 Table **E** shows the steps I took to find out about my house. Use the evidence on these pages to fill in the gaps.

E

Step	Source	Question	Answer
1	Library: books on Exeter	When was my house built?	
2	Library: maps of Exeter	Same	
3	Library: Census	Who lived there?	

2 List which of these sources are primary and which secondary.

3 Write a story about the building of my house, and what life might have been like inside it. To help you, use anything else you can find out about town life in the 1840s and '50s.

4 Use the ideas on these pages to research the history of your own house, or any other building.

HISTORY AROUND US: OUR SCHOOL

At what age did you start school?
What kind of school do you go to?
What are you taught?
How will this change as you get older?
How different are your answers from those that your parents and grandparents would have given?

As a class you can try to find out as much as possible about changes in *education* in the past hundred years. School textbooks contain many facts and ideas. **A** is taken from one.

A *... in 1870 an act was passed (by Parliament) which ordered the local councils to set up schools in places where there were not sufficient schools for the children. This does not mean that after 1870 every child went to school. In the first place the schools had to be built and the teachers had to be found. In 1891 all these schools were made free and attendance at them was compulsory.**

Other books in your school and local libraries will give you background facts. You can look for clues in several other places. At school you may find school photographs and written records. At your local record office you may discover more *primary sources* like the school diary or log book, kept from its earliest days. **B** is an extract from a first-hand source—a headmaster's diary—about school life from 1882-1900.

Another source is *what people remember* and tell you. **C** is a list of questions to ask your parents, grandparents, or an old friend or neighbour, about their schooldays. Before they—or you—put down the answers, you *must* show them the questionnaire first.

History means asking questions of the past. The deeper you get into a subject, the harder the questions become. From the work on our school, you can see that the questions are about the ideas on pages 6-11: why things happened, what happened, changes and consequences.

B *A headmaster's notes on changes in his Board School 1882-1900: The boy of 1900 as compared with the boy of 1880*

Cheerful and eager now, then often sullen and morose. Relations with teachers generally friendly, often affectionate—no streetcalling after them or stone throwing as there used to be. All this, the result of discipline and control at school, reacts beneficially at home. Truancy almost extinct and when occurring there is usually something in the blood to explain it. Theft rather common but perhaps more often detected owing to better supervision.

Personal cleanliness: Greatly improved: verminous cases among boys rare but among girls almost universal, due to their long hair. Out of thirty examined, twenty-eight required attention. As to dirt, it is necessary to distinguish between recent dirt got at play and the ancient kind that gives the strong smell. Swimming is taught and has a good effect. The really dirty, seen when stripped, would not be allowed to bathe, but would be sent home to wash first. This now seldom happens. The vermin referred to are lice; bugs are rarely seen: but fleas are common, especially on children coming from homes where there is a baby.

Obscene Language: Common both in the street and in the home, but not common in the school where, if disagreeable words are heard, they are checked.

Obscene Conduct: Very rare. As to boys and girls, the latter are the aggressors.

* A. M. Newith, *Britain and the World 1789-1901*

C SCHOOL QUESTIONNAIRE

NAME _____

1 Where did you go to school? (School's name, town, country)

2 Between which dates?

3 Which is your first memory of school life?

4 What is the oldest thing you can remember being told by anyone about school or their early life?

5 In your last year at school, what lessons did you have?

6 What major changes had there been in them over the years?

7 What books did you use?

8 What did you write on or in?

9 What other kind of work did you do—art, woodwork, metalwork etc?

10 What punishments were there?

11 Did the teachers use films, T.V., pictures, radio? If so, what can you remember of them?

12 Which was your most enjoyable lesson? Why?

13 Which was your least enjoyable lesson? Why?

14 Were there school meals? What were they like?

15 What important events took place at school? Describe one of them.

16 What did you do and wear for P.E., games?

17 How did you spend a typical day at school?

18 Did you go on school visits?

19 How did you travel to school? How far?

20 What stories can you remember about your school days which children today might like?

????????????????????????????

1 Write out **B** in your own words. Look up difficult words in the dictionary.

2 What does **B** tell you about how schoolchildren changed between 1870 and 1900? Can you explain these changes?

3 Use the class's answers to **C** to say how school life in your area has changed since 1900.

4 Make a plan of the steps you would take to research the history of your own school.

    a List the questions you would ask.
    b Say what kind of sources you would look at first, and where you might find them.
    c Say what kind of sources you would look at next, and where.
    d Say what kind of work you would hope to write at the end of your research.

HISTORY AROUND US: THE SECOND WORLD WAR

From 1939-45, Britain was at war with Germany. This war affected everyone's life. How would you find out about the impact of the war on the area where you live? **A—E** are clues about one day in the life of an English city, Exeter—3rd-4th May 1942.

History means asking questions about the clues or evidence which have survived from the past, and building up in your mind an idea of what happened.

A	Night and Date	Time	Bombs		Casualties		Extent of Damage
			Number	**Type**	**Killed**	**Wounded**	
	Sunday, Monday, 3rd-4th May	1.36 to 2.50 am	160	High Explosive, 75 tons in all	161	70 seriously	widespread
			about 10000	Incendiary bombs		406 slight	
			between 3 and 6	Paramines			

15 800 undamaged or slightly damaged

2 700 seriously damaged

1 500 destroyed

1 South Street
2 High Street
3 Sidwell Street
4 Paris Street
5 Southernhay
6 City Library
7 Telephone Exchange
8 Cathedral

■ Destroyed by bombs

30

D

HEART OF CITY 'BLITZED'

EXETER, ancient capital of the South-West, which in the early morning of April 25 was a victim of the Nazi so-called 'reprisal' raids, suffered a new raid this morning when in a period of an hour-and-a-half's intensive dive-bombing areas of the city were laid waste by high explosive and incendiary bombs.

This morning the raiders caused destruction in a shopping area, damaging and setting fire to blocks of property.

At the height of the attack the city was on fire in many parts, and several churches and other historic buildings were laid in ruins.

Countless Pitiful Scenes

It is feared that the loss of life will prove heavier than in the attack of nine days before, this second bombing attempt being on a considerably heavier scale.

Demolition of a great many houses, large or small, was wrought.

Through swirling flames and billowing clouds of acrid smoke, firemen made almost superhuman efforts in their attempts to limit the destruction. The police, warden, nursing services and Civil Defence workers also worked heroically

There were countless pitiful scenes typical of these hate raids. Old people and children removed such belongings as they could collect and made their way from shattered houses and damaged streets to the rest centres or to refuges with friends under the 'Help your Neighbour' scheme.

At one church high explosive bombs struck the tower, slicing half of it away and leaving some of the bells hanging in the open air from the belfry at the top.

School Gutted

A girls' school was gutted by fire following a shower of incendiaries and another school for girls was among the buildings struck.

Extensive damage was caused in another district when High Explosive and incendiary bombs rained down.

Many houses were wrecked and destructive fires started.

E

Pathetic Sight

'I went over to the hospital,' Mr Jones told our reporter. 'There were patients lying on the grass, and others walking towards a nearby building. It was a pathetic sight. The door of one building fronting the road must have been partly blown open by blast. One or two of the patients were being carried in. We cleared some debris at the bottom, and the students managed to lever the door completely open. I carried over a couple of patients and dashed into the playing field and asked for volunteers. A crowd of students came over with me. We used doors as stretchers and managed to fill the building except for three beds upstairs. These patients were evacuated the following afternoon.'

Hospital Hit

A hospital was burnt out and practically destroyed, but the inmates were evacuated. Nurses and staff worked heroically to effect the transfer, especially of the older patients and their devotion was beyond praise.

(*Express and Echo*, 4 May 1942)

??????????????????????????

1 Use **A—E** to answer these questions.
  a How many people were killed?
  b How many bombs fell?
  c What types were they?
  d How badly damaged were the houses?
  e What kinds of building did the Germans destroy?
  f Why did the Germans bomb Exeter?
  g What did Mr Jones say happened?
  h How soon after the raid was the report written in the *Express and Echo*?
  i Can we trust what it and Mr Jones tells us about the attack?

2 Use **A—E** to write your account of the raid on Exeter on 3rd-4th May, 1942. *Or* Imagine you were interviewing a policeman who was on duty during the raid.

3 Make up a questionnaire to ask people who lived through the Second World War what it was like.

4 List the possible sources that you would look at if you wanted to write a history of your nearest large city during the Second World War.

5 Why do you think no specific areas of Exeter were mentioned in **A** and **B**?

QUIZ TIME

All the answers can be found in this book

1. What did Miles Forest do with the pillow?
2. Where did the bombs fall?
3. How many people did they kill?
4. Where would you buy a goose?
5. Who is using the bellows, and why?
6. What ploughed the deep water?
7. Can you think what made a good impression?
8. Who had his throat cut?
9. Where can you find men walking on the moon?
10. How long did the Dark Ages last?
11. What is stuck in the anvil?
12. Is Cadbury Castle a castle?
13. What does BC mean?
14. Who were Richard and Edward?
15. Who got one in the eye?
16. What is a coin worth dated 43 BC?
17. What might have stood in the post-holes?
18. When did the school burn down?
19. What happened at Mount Badon?
20. In which century did the Second World War happen?
21. What is a primary source?
22. Who was not like Arthur?
23. Where can you find Queen Victoria keeping Hitler company?
24. What might the Duke of Buckingham have done?
25. What is a secondary source?
26. When did people in England first have to go to school?
27. What does the model show?
28. What did Ambrosius decide?
29. Who was he?
30. Who had fleas in 1880?
31. Who was Beowulf?
32. What did the Bromsgrove fire brigade do?
33. What did Professor Hoskins write?
34. When did the bombs drop?
35. Are the children enjoying their lesson?
36. Whom did Professor Glob come face to face with?
37. What is history?